Digital Marketing
Omni Channel Personalization

Sudhir Sreedharan

PREFACE

It is the job of marketing to create demand among qualified prospects in the target market, and drive them to the appropriate sales channel. Executives say their CEO's are more involved in digital efforts than ever before and that their enterprises are now investing enough to meet their overall digital goals. Current digital marketing efforts in companies are totally fragmented as it is all marketing channel driven. Every channel is in a race to maximize the sourced opportunities worsening the customer experience as a whole and in turn losing ground. This is just scratching the surface of this extremely evolving topic.

Omni channel personalization is all about being customer centric. What are you doing to move your organization in this direction and stay in the game?

Omni channel is not just a fancier name for multi channel. It represents a truly new methodology that is customer centric and non linear. It provides a seamless experience to the customer no matter the channel they interact with.

Marketing today is more about outcomes than interactions. Outcomes are what omni channel marketing is all about, putting the customer at the center of the brand experience so that engagement turns into revenue and loyalty. There are major people, process, and technology challenges with moving from multi channel to omni channel. This requires a real strategic focus and commitment.

In this day and age, there is a proliferation of channels and tactics and it is highly recommended that you, as a marketer, need to have a broad understanding of all of this. To learn more you need to understand channels to some level of detail before embarking upon omni channel personalization.

TABLE OF CONTENTS

1. Introduction to Digital Marketing   **7**
What is Digital Marketing   *8*
Why Digital Marketing   *10*
Growth of Digital Media   *13*
B2B Vs B2C Marketing   *14*
Inbound Vs Outbound Marketing   *16*
Multichannel Marketing   *17*
Conclusion   *17*

2. EMAIL Marketing   **20**
Introduction   *21*
Why Email Marketing   *22*
Email Best Practices   *23*
Email Marketing Tools   *26*
Conclusion   *27*

3. SEARCH Marketing   **28**
Introduction   *29*
Search Engine Optimization (SEO)   *30*
Search Engine Marketing (SEM)   *31*
Conclusion   *33*

4. WEB Marketing   **34**
Introduction   *35*
Key Performance Indicators   *37*
Display Advertising   *38*
Affiliate marketing   *39*
Web Syndication   *40*
Retargeting or Remarketing   *41*
Website Analytics Tools   *42*
A/B Vs MVT Testing   *43*
Conclusion   *44*

5. CONTENT Marketing   **46**
Introduction   *47*
Content Authoring Tools   *49*

Content Distribution Tools   *51*
Content Collaboration Tools   *52*
Globalization/Localization of Content   *53*
Localization tools   *53*
Conclusion   *54*

6. SOCIAL MEDIA Marketing   **55**
Introduction   *56*
Advantages of using social media   *57*
Risks of using social media   *58*
Blogging   *58*
Rise of social networks   *61*
Key social media services   *63*
Conclusion   *65*

7. MOBILE Marketing   **67**
Why Mobile Marketing   *68*
Location based marketing   *72*
Conclusion   *74*

8. Analytics   **75**
Introduction   *76*
Tracking the Data That Matters   *78*
Predictive Analytics   *79*
Conclusion   *81*

9. OMNI CHANNEL Personalization   **83**
Introduction   *84*
Buyer Journey/Customer Lifecycle   *85*
Personalization   *87*
Profile and Personas   *88*
Omni Channel   *91*
Business Architecture Approach   *94*
Measure the KPIs   *98*
Marketing to Sales   *100*
Conclusion   *101*

1. INTRODUCTION TO DIGITAL MARKETING

Contents

1. What is Digital Marketing
2. Why Digital Marketing
3. Growth of Digital Media
4. B2B Vs B2C Marketing
5. Inbound Vs Outbound Marketing
6. Multichannel Marketing
7. Conclusion

70% of business technology buyers are at the RFP stage by the time the vendor becomes aware of the opportunity.

For large technology purchases 7.2 decisions makers on average can touch or influence the decision.

By 2015, 71% of Marketing leads will come from the Web.

With the change and evolution of modern technologies, small and medium businesses are doing everything they can to keep up and be competitive. Similarly large businesses are also being innovative to keep up with the competition. Businesses of all sizes are adding online to their business models, or beefing up existing marketing efforts with digital marketing strategies in an attempt to capture a growing and very lucrative online marketplace.

Marketers are investing in the customer experience to drive business advantage and profitable revenue growth, according to a survey of marketing executives by Gartner, Inc. The survey found that marketing budgets remained healthy in 2014, with, on average, companies spending 10.2 percent of their annual 2014 revenue on overall marketing activities, with 50 percent of companies planning an increase in 2015.

For it is the process of attracting targeted audiences online that will spell the difference between a successfully thriving business and a failed one. Even if you receive tons of daily traffic to your website, they would not amount to anything unless they convert to leads or sales. In the digital arena where business and commerce are heading to, Digital Marketing tools and techniques provide business owners the best chances for competition, survival and business growth.

What is Digital Marketing

If you have ever googled this term "Digital Marketing" you would have been overwhelmed with the response you got from the web.

Try sending a gmail to someone or to yourselves about something, say "marketo", which is a marketing automation software company. Then, when you login to your facebook account, you see the ads related to Marketo. Aha !!! How did facebook know you are looking for Marketo ? This content was inside my, so called, secure email and how did it get out. Sounds intriguing ? Welcome to the world of Digital Marketing.

You would have read things like Digital marketing is all about content marketing - tailoring the content appropriately to the user persona ... it is all about personalizing the customer journey ... it is primarily search marketing - SEO/SEM ... it is about providing the ultimate web experience to the prospect ... mobility is taking the world by storm and it is all about mobile marketing ... it is data driven marketing ... it is being predictive ... social marketing is the next big wave .... display marketing, re-marketing or retargeting, tag management and on and on. This brings you to a totally confused state. While all of this is true, it is good for you as a technologist or executive to understand, how to get your arms around it, and what should you do to set a strategy and not be overwhelmed with these disparate processes, tools and technologies.

Marketing has been around forever and has always been for generating demand and awareness. The traditional ways of marketing has been news paper ads, flyers, magazines, posters & banners, events, door to door marketing, word of mouth, radio ads, television ads etc. In this day and age with the explosion of digital, there are lot more ways highly effective and cheaper to reach the masses.

Digital Marketing, in simple terms, is the promotion of your products, services or your brand via one or more forms of digital or electronic media.

There is a proliferation of digital media and day by day we see intuitive ways of marketing. Some of these include channels like email which is still extremely popular, web, search marketing, mobile, social media and so on. The rest of this book goes into some level of detail for you to understand what does all this mean and how can you be more informed.

Why Digital Marketing

The newspaper industry has always been cyclical, and the industry has weathered previous troughs. But with television's arrival in the 1950s presaged the decline of newspapers' importance as most people's source of daily news, the explosion of the internet in the 1990s and the first decade of the 21st century increased the collection of media choices available to the average reader while further cutting into newspapers' dominance as the source of news. Both television and the Internet bring news to the consumer faster and in a more visual style than newspapers, which are constrained by their physical form and the need to be physically manufactured and distributed. The competing mediums also offer advertisers the opportunity to use moving images and sound. And the internet search function allows advertisers to tailor their pitch to readers who have revealed what information they are seeking an enormous advantage.

The decline of newspapers has been widely debated as the industry has faced down soaring newsprint prices, slumping ad sales, the loss of much classified advertising and precipitous drops in circulation. In recent years the number of newspapers slated for closure, bankruptcy or severe cutbacks has risen especially in the United States, where the industry has shed a fifth of its journalists since 2001. Revenue has plunged while competition from internet media has squeezed older print publishers. Newspapers are going out of business if they do not have an online digital presence because people like you and me are not buying them anymore but rather relying on the internet to provide you the customized news content per your interest at your convenience and device of choice.

With a number of states now offering schools the option of purchasing digital content and equipment with funds previously earmarked for textbooks, some are predicting the demise of the print textbook as we know it today. How likely is this? And how desirable? K-12 textbooks cost the state of California over $400 million/year according to the California Open Source Textbook Project. Between 1986 and 2004 college textbook prices nearly tripled. Our kids are sitting in front of computers to do their homework. How many of college going kids today are looking forward to print media as against watching video of the same content or listening to audio and that too while going for a run or commuting to school or waiting for someone. Today, you can specialize on any topic by sitting with a laptop and an internet connection and not spending a dime, then why would someone want to buy print media.

You will not find any advertisement on flyers, newspapers, magazines, door to door marketing, word of mouth, televisions, radios etc without the mention of the online media information. In other words today, if at all, print media or other non digital media is all about driving traffic to the online digital media. It is high time we realize this and focus our time and money on this digital media or we will be run over by other businesses who are doing that more efficiently.

You will also be surprised to find that lot of this comes at a lower expense and faster time to market than the print media.

Many organizations aren't doing enough with digital technologies to maximize the impact of marketing, according to a recent survey from Wipro Limited and Forbes Insights. You'd think that IT would be considered a prime candidate for input and support here, but many executives said the technology department is too busy to provide much help. "Executives today face a bewildering array of digital marketing technologies," says Hiral Chandrana, vice president and global business head of consumer goods for Wipro Limited. "It not only requires integrated Website, mobile and social media strategies ... but also concepts such as omni-channel and analytics, which add to the complexity. Below are findings based on a research from 125 C-level executives representing a wide range of consumer goods companies

65% of C-level execs surveyed said their firms must do more to harness digital technology to improve marketing efficiencies

42% of them said their current approach to digital marketing is too fragmented

50% of execs believe that their digital marketing has failed to integrate with essential back-end processes

59% said their companies are amenable to employing more tech outsourcing so a third party IT provider can help with front-end marketing and back-end operational processes.

In almost all walks of lives people are moving from the traditional ways to digital, be it from reading news papers and articles to buying groceries to buying houses to anything and everything. People out there do lot of research before they come up with their options. What does this mean ? Is it that they are close to making a decision even before they approach you ? In B2B, 70% of the purchase decision is made before talking to the company. If so, what is it that you can do to influence them early on and how can you provide them an ultimate experience that make them trusted advisors of your product or service.

Growth of Digital Media

Digital is the only media channel predicted to grow in the next 3 years according to Zenith Optimedia. It is now #2 behind TV. By the end of the decade, many expect is to be ahead of TV. A decade ago, it was just beginning to make an appearance.

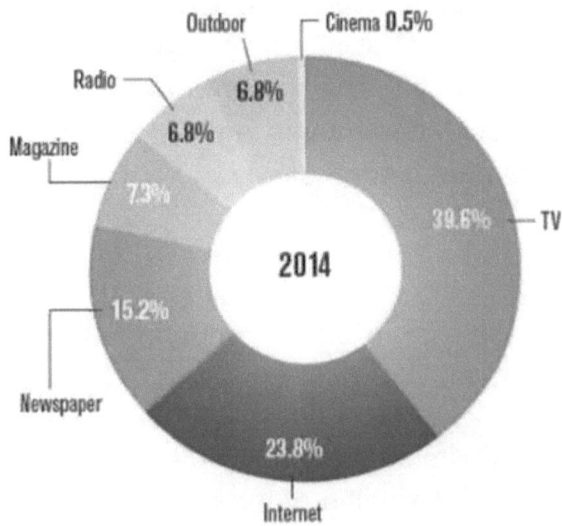

WORLDWIDE AD SPENDING BY MEDIUM

Worldwide major-media total
in 2014: $519.9 billion, up 5.1%.

Executives say their CEO's are more involved in digital efforts than ever before and that their enterprises are now investing enough to meet their overall digital goals.

It is the job of marketing to create demand among qualified prospects in the target market, and drive them to the appropriate sales channel.

B2B Vs B2C Marketing

In order to level set on some of this terminology used across let us understand what they mean and how they impact. Marketing & Selling to Businesses (B2B - Business to

Business) and to end consumers (B2C - Business to Consumer) are different in many ways and common in some others. If you look at Amazon whose target is consumers like you and me, as against, like a Cisco, who targets businesses you will understand some of the differences. When you need to purchase anything first you go to amazon.com to check out the price of the product, reviews and so on whereas if you need a router or a switch, which in itself is highly unlikely, you will not go to Cisco.com to see if you can buy that. You might still go to amazon to find the router you want to purchase. In other words these companies need to understand their prospects and market it accordingly.

B2C Vs B2B

- B2C purchase is product driven, whereas B2B is relationship driven

- In B2C, you maximize the value of the transaction whereas in B2B maximize the value of the relationship

- B2C has a large target market but for B2B it is a small, focused target market.

- B2C has a shorter sales cycle as compared to B2B.

- B2C Brand identity is created through repetition and imagery where B2B uses personal relationship

- B2C has an emotional buying decision based on status, desire or price whereas B2B has a rational buying decision based on business value.

These characteristics have significant impact on how you market and who you market to.

Inbound Vs Outbound Marketing

Inbound marketing focuses on creating quality content that pulls people toward your company and product whereas Outbound marketing, mostly traditional marketing, is the marketing we grew up with: radio, TV, newspapers, magazines, direct-mail, billboards, event sponsorships, etc with exception of email and some others.

- 45% of direct mail never gets opened

- 200 million people are on the national Do Not Call Registry

- 85% of people fast forward through TV commercials

- 84% of 25--35 year-olds are likely to click off a website with excessive advertising

- 91% unsubscribe from emails

Inbound marketing is permission-based marketing. There are two premises here.

First, communicate via mediums in which the audience has given you permission to communicate. Examples: subscription based email marketing, social media, blog subscribers, webinar attendees, etc.

Second, answer the questions people are asking and proliferate those answers around the web in anticipation of the question. Examples: SEO, keyword targeting, landing page strategy, content/blog strategy, etc.

Per Hubspot,

- Inbound creates 54% more leads than outbound.

- Inbound costs 61% less than outbound. Outbound average cost per lead is $346 whereas inbound cost per lead is only $135.

- Inbound marketing channels cost less than any outbound marketing channel.

Multichannel Marketing

Multichannel marketing refers to the practice of marketing to customers using a combination of indirect and direct communication channels – websites, retail stores, mail order catalogs, direct mail, email, social, mobile, etc. Multichannel marketing is important for the simple reason that you must be where your customers are and you need to interact with the customer's in their preferred way to be most effective.

There's no doubt that customers today have much more control over the buying process than marketers do. Thanks to the proliferation of available channels, customers have more choices than ever when it comes to how they want to get information.

Conclusion

To reiterate, Digital Marketing, in simple terms, is the promotion of your products, services or your brand via one or more forms of digital or electronic media.

B2C purchase is product driven, whereas B2B is relationship driven. 84% of 25—35 year-olds are likely to click off a website with excessive advertising. Inbound marketing costs 61% less than outbound. Digital is the only media channel predicted to grow in the next 3 years.

Some of the key aspects of digital marketing :

1. Create demand - not simply spew information about your product, but to speak in terms of customer problems, needs, and desires. To start with THEIR perspective.

2. Qualified prospects - your pipeline stays clean when marketing does its job of targeting and filtering appropriately. Don't make sales clean up after you.

3. Target market – spend your money reaching people who might care. Coverage does not equal effectiveness.

4. Drive – your job isn't over once you get their attention. You must continue to compel them relentlessly towards engaging with your sales team, qualifying and weeding out as you go, so that sales gets an edible product.

No matter the tactic used to acquire prospects, the key is take it through the process to finally get it converted and realize revenue.

Per Gartner, the top 3 challenges for marketers in 2015 are growth, competition and connecting with customers. Mobile marketing and digital advertising will see the highest digital spend increase in 2015, followed by analytics and social marketing.

All that said, now you as a marketer need to understand these marketing channel with some level of detail before creating strategies and tactics for your company.

2. EMAIL MARKETING

Contents

1. Introduction
2. Why Email Marketing
3. Email Best Practices
4. Email Marketing Tools
5. Conclusion

85 percent of US retailers consider email marketing one of the most effective customer acquisition tactics.

Introduction

One of the common things in this day and age is being continuously spammed by email from different vendors. Emails can be used in other ways too.

The other day I was on one of the hardly known eCommerce sites adding a couple of things to my cart. I then started looking for coupons that, I thought, I had, but could not find them and was in two minds on placing the order. I stepped away and came back after an hour or so, only to find an email from that vendor with a 10% off coupon. I immediately went ahead and completed the order. This is also the power of Email.

Email can constantly help in nurturing the customer to get business. It is also about knowing the customer well in advance to personalize the message based on his/her interest. No matter the tactic you use, the goal is to convert the lead or opportunity to a successful business transaction which in most cases is an order.

Per Wikipedia, Email marketing is directly marketing a commercial message to a group of people using email. In its broadest sense, every email sent to a potential or current customer could be considered email marketing. It usually involves using email to send ads, request business, or solicit sales or donations, and is meant to build loyalty, trust, or brand awareness.

Like any marketing channel, email is also targeted to specific user segments based on their relationship with the company, their demographics, firmographics and their propensity to purchase the specific product or service.

Why Email Marketing

Email is by far the most effective way of directly affecting your bottom line and actually growing your business. Even though technology has significantly improved with instant messaging and social media, people still rely on emails for a number of things.

Some of the key reasons why Email Marketing still works :

Email is an easy way to reach mobile customers. While texting incurs charge, email is free. Email also has more space for content not that you need to have a long message.

It's an effective way to keep customers informed. Customers do in most cases opt for receiving emails from their preferred stores to get discounts and promotions. A 2013 study by the Relevancy Group noted that marketers who add video to their email campaigns see an average rise in revenue of 40 percent. A study from Loyalty 360 stated that 59 percent of US moms would sign up for email updates from brands if rewards were offered.

Email coupons drive online and in-store sales. The Nielsen study also found that 27 percent of US online shoppers subscribe to store or product emails in order to save money. Shop.org reported 64 percent of US Internet users have printed a coupon from an email.

It's easy to customize and integrate into other marketing tactics. A small study of 139 marketers from Retention Science found that websites use several kinds of personalization tactics that can easily be applied to email. Nearly half of US online retailers used personalized product recommendations (44.9%), about a third added the customer's name and/or a unique welcome message (31.5%), and a quarter of the respondents reported adding shopping cart reminders (27.6%) to cover all of their personalization bases.

Email marketing is inexpensive. To sum up the best reason to use email marketing: It's easy, effective, and inexpensive. A joint study from Shop.org and Forrester Research found that 85 percent of US retailers consider email marketing one of the most effective customer acquisition tactics.

The point of all this is that email may be an old tactic, but it remains a vital one. It's relatively easy to get started with email marketing, so there's no excuse for business owners to not be taking advantage of this tactic.

By the way, a significant percent of all email messages are rejected or filtered out. Companies considering the use of an email marketing program must make sure that their program does not violate spam laws such as the United States' Controlling the Assault of Non-Solicited Pornography and Marketing Act (CAN-SPAM), the European Privacy and Electronic Communications Regulations 2003, or their Internet service provider's acceptable use policy.

Email Best Practices

Email Subject Line :

- Get To The Point - Under 35 characters or 4-6 words in length. Keep most important detail towards the front.

- Does it Communicate Email Content? - Subject line should sum up the content of your email

- Is Value Proposition Clear? - In addition to summing up the copy within, the subject line should always include the value proposition. What will the recipient get by reading this email?

- Does It Motivate? - Subject lines with action words, urgency or numbered lists persuade the reader to take action.

- Did You Avoid... - Spam words, capital letters and "Company Name" in the subject line?

- Does Your Subject Line Stand Out? - Most email recipients open their inbox, scan the 'From Line' and then Subject Line, and then decide if they will delete. How does your email stand out among the rest? Is your value proposition unique?

- Did You Test your Subject Line? - How did your subject line look in different email clients and devices?

Email Layout :

- Take Advantage of Valuable Real-Estate? - The top left corner of the email is very visible. This area should contain the CTA and most important details.

- Imagery - How does your email look with images off? Do the images display correctly? Is alternate text being used? Do the images support the value proposition?

- Is Your Email Mobile Friendly? - The number one way people access the internet is through their mobile devices. Optimize the layout for smart phones.

- Testing? - How do the headers, images, and links perform across different email clients and devices?

Email Copy :

The Recipient Is Scanning the Email - Many recipients only scan the email. Get your message out in as few words as possible. Keep it simple and easier to scan.

CTA Placement & Quantity - Keep the CTA and pertinent detail towards the top of the email above the fold. It is best to have a single CTA per email but provide multiple opportunities via buttons, linkable images and text links.

Tone - Speak Human – don't speak corporate. Write for the recipient and not yourself. Does your copy answer the question: "What's in it for me?"

Bullets & Numbered Lists (ordered lists) - Bullets and numbered lists can be valuable if used properly.

Proofing Your Email Copy - Be in charge of the copy that you submit regardless if you authored it or someone else did. Proof it for grammar, spelling and overall tone. Ensure that the products are properly branded and the language meets the company standards.

According to Yesware's analysis of over 500,000 sales emails sent in Q1 2014, email open and reply rates are higher on the weekends. Why? It could be because there's significantly less email being sent on weekends.

Email Reply Rates are Highest on the Weekends

	Emails Sent	% Open	% Reply	% Reply Same Day
Week Day	525,742	66.3%	39.1%	33.1%
Weekend	5,278	73.6%	45.8%	32.6%

Email Marketing Tools

Some of the popular email marketing tools excluding marketing automation tools like marketo, eloqua etc :

Constant Contact – Design professional-looking emails, grow and manage your email list, and track results. In addition to email, Constant Contact offers tools for social campaigns, online surveys, and more.

iContact – Create HTML emails and signup forms, send campaigns to customers inboxes, track email campaigns, and more. iContact also offers social social media marketing tools.

Campaign Monitor – Customize your email template, send campaigns, conduct A/B testing, integrate with your blog, and more.

Conclusion

Email marketing is significantly cheaper and faster than traditional mail, mainly because of high cost and time required in a traditional mail campaign for producing the artwork, printing, addressing and mailing. Advertisers can reach substantial numbers of email subscribers who have opted in (i.e., consented) to receive email communications on subjects of interest to them. Almost half of American Internet users check or send email on a typical day. Video on your email campaigns will see an average potential rise in revenue of up to 40 percent.

To summarize, 85 percent of US retailers consider email marketing one of the most effective customer acquisition tactics and keep in mind email is by far the most effective way of directly affecting your bottom line and actually growing your business.

3. SEARCH MARKETING

Contents

1. Introduction
2. Search Engine Optimization (SEO)
3. Search Engine Marketing (SEM)
4. Conclusion

85% of all web traffic comes via search engines including Google, Bing and Yahoo!.

Being listed on these sites is crucial to the success of your business.

Introduction

Search marketing is the process of gaining traffic and visibility from search engines through both paid and unpaid efforts. Broadly, the unpaid or free ways of doing this is considered SEO and the paid efforts are categorized as SEM, Search Engine Marketing.

Search engines are pervasive. They are on cell-phones, iPads, tablets, netbooks, laptops and desktop computers. We use the Internet to make every day decisions, such as where to eat, where to shop and which businesses and brands to trust. Search is everywhere. The key for business is to be positioned in front of people making those searches, and its not just about high rankings for your company name. There is infinitely more potential for your business with search.

Studies have revealed that search engine users overwhelmingly click on organic results on Google and Bing by a margin of 94 percent to 6 percent. Others have previously tried to gauge organic click-through rates (CTRs) for the top 10 results on Google and Bing, resulting in varied percentages, but with a recurring and obvious theme: the higher you rank, the more people click on your website, the lower you rank, the less clicks and traffic your site gets. Thus, ranking high on Page 1 is of ultimate value to every website.

SiriusDecisions reports that 70% of the buying process in a complex sale is already complete before prospects are willing to engage with a live salesperson. Lot of this comes through online search for most B2C transactions.

Search Engine Optimization (SEO)

Per wikipedia, Search engine optimization (SEO) is the process of affecting the visibility of a website or a web page in a search engine's "natural" or un-paid ("organic") search results. All major search engines such as Google, Yahoo and Bing have search results, where web pages and other content such as videos or local listings are shown and ranked based on what the search engine considers most relevant to users. When a user searches for some keywords, there are a number of ways you can make these search engines show your site on the top of the search results. Some of Optify's findings a couple of years back which depicts the importance of being on the top of all the search results :

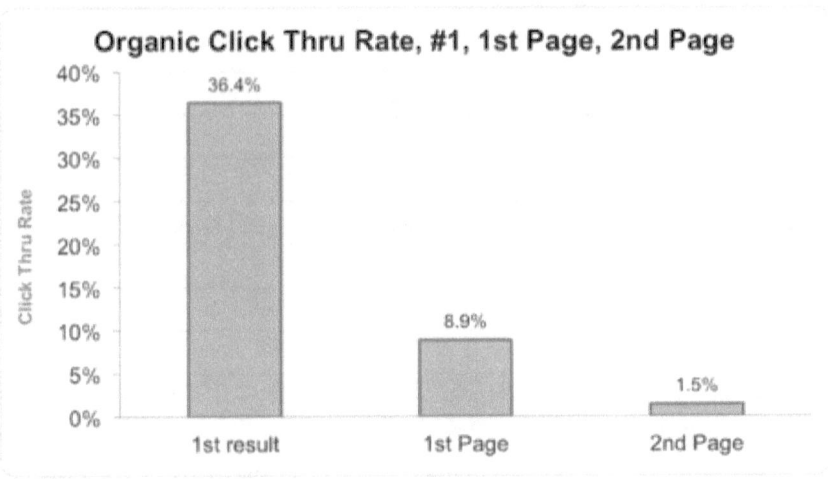

The million dollar question is how do you get to the top of the search results. There are a number of companies out there whose business model is all about helping you come to the top of the search results. There are dos and don'ts. There are ways of doing it like have you researched the keywords people may use to find your content, making sure the html title contains the keywords relevant to the page topic, does the site load quickly and so forth. SearchEngineLand.com is one of those popular search marketing sites that has done a good job at summarizing the dos and don'ts. Checkout this periodic table of SEO success factors from Search Engine Land.

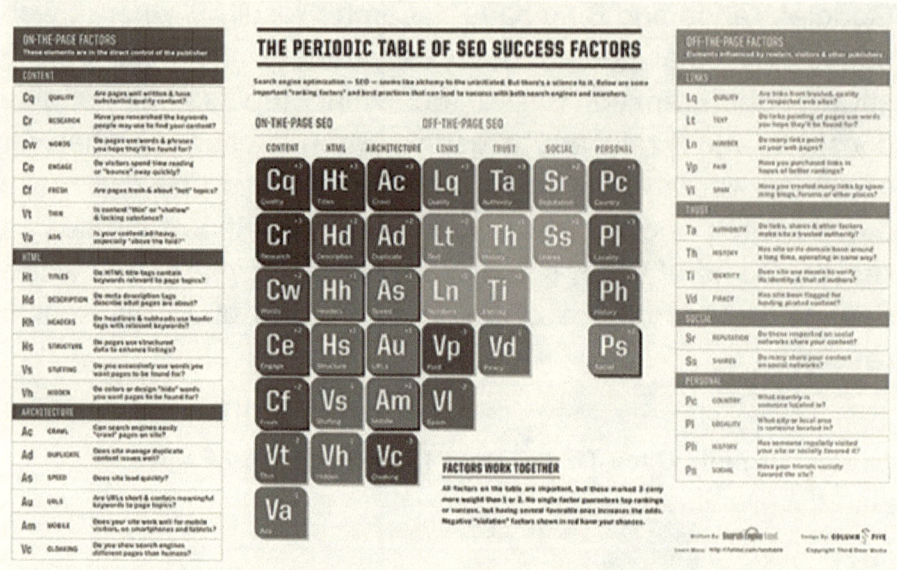

This is a very good table to keep handy. They have more details on tips and tutorials about implementing on their site.

Also keep in mind this is an evolving area since the search engines can make changes to their logic and that can have a different effect on your SEO efforts. But following the above will at least address things more closely to getting your site up there on the search results.

Search Engine Marketing (SEM)

SEM is the process of gaining traffic by purchasing ads on search engines. It is also called paid search and sometimes referred to as CPC (cost-per-click) or PPC (pay-per-click) marketing, because most search ads are sold on a CPC / PPC basis. Search engine marketing, was once used as an umbrella term to encompass both SEO (search engine optimization) and paid search activities, however, over time, many adopted the SEM acronym to refer solely to paid search.

Pay-per-click (PPC) search engines can give you instant traffic and allow you to test new business models in real time. However, the pay-per-click market is competitive. It is worth spending an extensive period of time learning how to write and target ads, tracking your competitors, and doing deep keyword research before jumping in. Pay-per-click search engines allow you to be listed at the top of search results quickly, which allows you to:

- Quickly gather feedback on market conditions.

- Split test a live audience and gather ad test results in real time.

- Prototype ideas to track demand before you invest into a new business model or are stuck footing the bill for a new site.

As an example of the power of PPC, you can use Google AdWords to offer a free white paper about a topic from a one-page website. If nobody is interested in downloading your white paper, or you cannot seem to get enough click-throughs, then that could indicate one or several things:

- You are not bidding high enough to get exposure.

- The market is not yet ready for your product.

- You are marketing it from the wrong angle.

- Your landing page is not making a compelling offer.

- You are marketing it to the wrong people.

When opening up a PPC accounts, many people are hesitant to spend a lot of money. In spending a small amount, the business is essentially ignoring the feedback loops search engines have set up.

Is it better to lose $100 today, or to lose it over three months and finally come to the conclusion that you need to change?

Conclusion

85% of all web traffic comes via search engines including Google, Yahoo! and Bing. Being listed on these sites is crucial to the success of your business. Search engine marketing is the easiest and most transparent way to help your online success, reaching and increasing qualified traffic to your website. The search challenge for most businesses is to generate qualified leads, consistently and at a reasonable cost of acquisition while improving revenue and brand awareness. Make sure to maximize all SEO tactics before getting into paid search.

4. WEB MARKETING

Contents

1. Introduction

2. Key Performance Indicators

3. Display Advertising

4. Affiliate marketing

5. Web Syndication

6. Retargeting Or Remarketing

7. Website Analytics Tools

8. A/B Vs MVT Testing

9. Conclusion

71% of Marketing leads will come from the Web. 67% of Buyer Journey is now online

Introduction

It really depends how you define web marketing.

Web Marketing is the marketing capability delivered through the web, that includes and is not limited to, company's main website, the landing web page for email/search campaigns, web user experience for online user, company ecommerce and other websites, display advertising that is located on third party websites, affiliate marketing that drives customers and revenue for the company, web syndication of content and other web site related activities.

Why is the web significant for marketing :

71% of Marketing leads will come from the Web

67% of Buyer Journey is now online

- A CEB (Corporate Executive Board) study of more than 1,400 B2B customers found that those customers completed, on average, nearly 60% of a typical purchasing decision – researching solutions, ranking options, setting requirements, benchmarking pricing, and so on – before even having a conversation with a supplier..

- For large technology purchases 7.2 decisions makers on average can touch or influence the decision.

The hardest thing about B2B selling today is that customers don't need you the way they used to per Harvard Business Review.

Two-thirds to 90% of the buying cycle is completed before a B2B buyer ever speaks with a sales rep. – Forrester. Your challenge is how do you influence your potential customers before even you are aware of them.

Business buyers spend just 21% of buying cycle in conversations with salespeople, instead spending 23% of the time in conversations with peers and colleagues and 56% of the buying cycle searching for and engaging with content – IDG Connect

70% of business technology buyers are at the RFP stage (request for proposal) by the time the vendor becomes aware of the opportunity per UBM Techweb.

What we have seen is most companies tend to start their online presence with a .com web site only too soon to realize they need lot of other capabilities some of which are provided through SaaS vendors and some with custom in house development making the enterprise systems landscape extremely complex. This causes a fragmented experience for the customer be it marketing or an end to end user experience. Lots of web capabilities, each might look good on its own but lacks the collective strategy on where to take the customer through their journey.

Most companies lack basic capabilities like SSO (Single Sign On), have disparate look and feel across their web properties, have no common infrastructure causing a lack of an integrated experience, have no way to identify cross sell/up sell opportunities to name a few.

Key Performance Indicators

KPIs are measures that help you understand how you are doing against your objectives. Reiterating, **measure** your

objectives.

Google Analytics has become the de-facto champion for free web analytics. Google Analytics can monitor dozens of KPIs for your business' web analytics KPIs, which refer to website traffic and visitor behavior, analyze all available web data with the purpose of understanding and improving web usage.

Here are the top five categories of Google Analytics KPIs every company should focus :

- Visits (Sessions), Unique Visitors (Users) and New vs Returning Visitors

- Traffic Sources : How people find your website is an invaluable metric to measure with Google Analytics. Visitors come from different "sources" including:

  Organic Search (google, bing, yahoo)

  Paid Search (CPC) (google adwords, yahoo search marketing)

  Referral (visitors that came via direct links on other websites)

  Social (Twitter, Facebook, Google+)

  Newsletter

  Direct Traffic (users that typed in your URL directly)

- Page Tracking: Bounce Rate and Average Session Duration by Channel. Bounce Rate is the percentage of single-page sessions (i.e. sessions in which the person left your site from the entrance page without interacting with the page). These Google Analytics KPIs indicate whether your visitors find what they are looking for on your website or if they leave your site immediately.

- Goal Conversion Tracking: Conversions and Conversion Rate by Channel. Conversion means different things for different parts of your website. Signing up for an email newsletter or making a purchase can both be counted as a conversion.

- Cost per Conversion, Profit and ROI (Return on Investment) by Channel. A poor ROI or cost per conversion can signify ineffective marketing activities. Tracking what channels the conversions are coming from helps narrow down problem areas and proves what channels are yielding the best results.

Display Advertising

Display advertising is graphical advertising on the World Wide Web that appears next to content on web pages, IM applications, email, etc.

These ads, often referred to as banners, come in standardized ad sizes, and can include text, logos, pictures, or more recently, rich media.

Google, a leader in the display ad network, lets you

1. Create all types of ads - text, image, interactive and video ads.

2. Place those ads on websites that are relevant to what

you're selling.

3. Show those ads to the people that are likely to be most interested.

4. Manage and track your budget, campaigns and results as you go.

Similarly there are other display ad networks that you can leverage for your business. Google is the most popular out of those.

Affiliate marketing

Per Wikipedia, Affiliate marketing is a type of performance-based marketing in which a business rewards one or more affiliates for each visitor or customer brought by the affiliate's own marketing efforts.

This is a win-win situation for both companies. There are a number of companies who provide a mechanism or widget that can be easily integrated into your website and the affiliate's website. These brokers do all tracking for billing and payments making it easy for companies to work together.

Affiliate marketing overlaps with other Internet marketing methods to some degree, because affiliates often use regular advertising methods. Those methods include organic search engine optimization (SEO), paid search engine marketing (PPC - Pay Per Click), e-mail marketing, content marketing and in some sense display advertising.

Web Syndication

Per Wikipedia, Web syndication is a form of syndication in

which website material is made available to multiple other sites. Most commonly, web syndication refers to making web feeds available from a site in order to provide other people with a summary or update of the website's recently added content (for example, the latest news or forum posts).

Syndication refers to the websites providing information and the websites displaying it. For the receiving site, content syndication is an effective way of adding greater depth and immediacy of information to its pages, making it more attractive to users. For the transmitting site, syndication drives exposure across numerous online platforms.

You can have your channel partners be provided packaged content of your product marketing which they display on their site and the syndication of this content is managed by your company.   With minimal time and hassle, content is seamlessly and automatically updated on a regular basis across the entire partner channel network.

There are a number of vendor companies who provide frameworks for web syndication like ShareVue or StructuredWeb.

Retargeting or Remarketing

Retargeting, also known as remarketing, is a form of online advertising that can help you keep your brand in front of bounced traffic after they leave your website. For most websites, only 2% of web traffic converts on the first visit. Retargeting is a tool designed to help companies reach the 98% of users who don't convert right away.

Retargeting is a cookie-based technology that uses simple

Javascript code to anonymously 'follow' your audience all over the Web.

Here's how it works: you place a small, unobtrusive piece of code on your website (this code is sometimes referred to as a pixel). The code, or pixel, is unnoticeable to your site visitors and won't affect your site's performance. Every time a new visitor comes to your site, the code drops an anonymous browser cookie. Later, when your cookied visitors browse the Web, the cookie will let your retargeting provider know when to serve ads, ensuring that your ads are served to only to people who have previously visited your site.

Retargeting is a powerful branding and conversion optimization tool, but it works best if it's part of a larger digital strategy.

Tool for Retargeting :

Resonance – This tool retargets content for your audience, and keeps your messaging in front of them, by tracking what your site visitors are viewing and making them aware of more relevant content.

Website Analytics Tools

Some of the good website analytics tools :

Kissmetrics – This ecommerce customer intelligence tool person-centric data in real time and ties anonymous activity to known activity once a visitor becomes a customer.

Google Analytics – Google's web analytics tool allows companies to customize reports, measure the impact of social media and mobile on website traffic, and measure conversion rates.

Webtrends – This digital marketing company offers tools for measuring and optimizing digital campaigns. Webtrends offers analytic intelligence including customer intelligence and behavioral segmentation, targeting and scoring, and more.

Mixpanel – Instead of measuring pageviews, this analytics tool measures actions such as searches or shares to gain greater insights into user behavior.

Woopra – Using real-time stats that can be broken down to an individual-level view, Woopra helps brands tracks visitors across multiple devices and build comprehensive timelines for every user.

Docalytics – Cloud-based platform that allows departments across a company to view documents, review analytics and track leads.

Simplereach – By collecting real-time data, this tool helps track the impact of digital content and allows users to gain insight into what direction they should take their created content strategy.

A/B Vs MVT Testing

A/B testing, is a method of website optimization in which the conversion rates of two versions of a page — version A and version B — are compared to one another using live traffic. By tracking the way visitors interact with the page they are shown the videos they watch, the buttons they click, or whether or not they sign up for a newsletter, you can determine which version of the page is most effective. A/B testing is the least complex method of evaluating a page design, and is useful in a variety of situations.

Multivariate testing (MVT) uses the same core mechanism as A/B testing, but compares a higher number of variables, and reveals more information about how these variables interact with one another. As in an A/B test, traffic to a page is split between different versions of the design. The purpose of a multivariate test, then, is to measure the effectiveness each design combination has on the ultimate goal.

Don't let the differences between A/B testing and multivariate testing make you think of them as opposites. Instead, think of them as two powerful optimization methods that complement one another. Pick one or the other, or use them both together to help you get the most out of your site.

Conclusion

Over and above the tools mentioned earlier, there are a few more tools that could be of interest to you :

Responsinator.com to emulate your site on different devices.

Looktracker.com conducts usability eye tracking focus group studies to provide highly accurate eye tracking heat map reports specific to your web page. Use the data to increase conversions and improve the user experience of a site.

Compete.com for monitoring online competition and benchmarking their performance compared to you.

Checkdog.com for spell checker

Google Ad preview & Diagnostics, so you do not use your

adwords budget that does not create impressions.

Google also offers a wide range of tools and resources to help developers build faster websites via https://developers.google.com/speed/pagespeed/insights/

KISSMetrics reported that 47 percent of users expect a page to load within two seconds. You can use Pingdom or GTMetrix, which are great tools for testing site speed.

Create a consistent and extensible set of responsive page layout guidelines that allow for all content types across sites. Update pages to new guidelines as needed. Target content to specific personas or prioritize them via design.

Website user experience should strategically focus on the following aspects.

Simplicity: Allow easy access to information through a self-guiding interface

Relevance: Tailor messaging to the target audiences

Branding: Tell your brand story in a believable way

Relationship Building: Provide lasting value, which drives long-term engagement

Purpose: Lead the audience to complete specific tasks

Personalize the entire web experience be it on the .com site or the ecommerce site, training & education site, knowledge base, etc. And later you can learn more about omni channel personalization which is ideally the way to go.

Per Avinask Kaushik, Digital Marketing Evangelist, you might want to ask 3 questions to your web user as he/she is leaving the site :

What is the purpose of your visit to our website today?

Were you able to complete your task today?

If you were not able to complete your task today, why not?

This survey will provide you interesting insights to provide a better user experience.

5. CONTENT MARKETING

Contents

1. Introduction
2. Content Authoring Tools
3. Content Distribution Tools
4. Content Collaboration Tools
5. Globalization/Localization of Content
6. Conclusion

70+ % of the content is always unused causing more clutter and distractions from the useful content.

A research study has found the annual growth rate of content production to be 200%.

Introduction

Marketing is impossible without great content. Regardless of what type of marketing tactics you use, content marketing should be part of your process, not something separate. Quality content is part of all channels of marketing be it Email, Social, Search etc.

Content marketing is marketing that involves the creation and sharing of media and publishing content in order to acquire and retain customers. You ideally need content strategists to plan and manage the content. You can see that content is core to marketing. The goal of content is to captivate the customer to reading the content and leading to the Call To Action based on the message.

Content can be in the form of product marketing assets, whitepapers, videos, web page content, email marketing content, display ad content, blogs and so on. The same product or service might be marketed through multiple channels and the content needs to be customized accordingly. You could be tweeting about your new product which is a 140 char text or you could have a 5 min youtube video being posted or you could have a product brochure created for circulation to prospects and all of these will have different content even though the product is the same. This requires specialized skill in generating the content.

A research study has found the annual growth rate of content production to be 200%. With so many people creating so much content, there will be more emphasis and commitment to generating meaningful content that is highly targeted on the goal of making deeper connections. Even though the amount of content will continue to rise, that doesn't mean that the content put forth will work for all brands. Since the future will require standing out with better, more targeted content, only the brands that produce content with the targeted audience in mind will benefit from the content boom that will have many people craving something different.

Once upon a time, written content was king, but times have changed. With mobile use increasing at such substantial rates, there are now more than 100 million consumers watching online video each day. This is precisely why brands need to have alternatives to written content. Video is an alternative that lends itself well to the mobile age, and that is why in 2015, we are going to see more video than we have seen before. As brands recognize the need to use video to reach their audience, explanatory videos, video-based storytelling, and video-embedded content will be hot.

By the way, a significant percentage like 70+ of the content is always unused. This causes more clutter and distractions from the useful content so it is highly desirable to manage the content more closely. You might want to tighten up your processes to manage the content using some content management tools. When some aspect of a product gets updated you need to reflect that update across all the relevant content and in some cases managing multiple versions based on the channels and device.

The below image from curata.com does nicely provide the content marketing tools available to online marketers

Tool for Content Marketing :

Idio – Improve content marketing strategy by examining specific customer interests and increasing the engagement of content.

Content Authoring Tools

Easelly – Using a theme-based approach to creating infographics and visualizations this online tool, lets users drag and drop art into a theme to create shareable graphics.

Visual.ly – Browse infographics and data visualizations and create your own to drive traffic to your brand's website and amplify your social media presence.

Adobe Creative Cloud – Sync and organize your creative assets across multiple devices, track comments, build and publish websites, apps, and more.

KnowledgeVision – Turn presentations and web content into an integrated, interactive online video experience that doesn't require special software or app downloads.

Brainshark – Sync up marketing and sales people using a systematic, coordinated approach in this content-centric sales platform.

Prezi – This presentation tool helps users organize and share ideas by creating visualizations.

Lookbook HQ – Using your most relevant, compelling content, this tool compiles all the information you want to display to customers into a visually appealing lookbook that can be embedded or shared.

Uberflip - This tool pulls all of your content; articles, social channels, videos, into a single centralized content hub.

Zmags – This platform helps e-commerce users create and share online catalogs, lookbooks, magazines, etc. to increase consumer engagement.

infogr.am – This tools helps users create interactive infographics. Users can edit data, download infographics and share & embed them.

Piktochart - This tool provides infographic templates for users and helps them create and share compelling content.

Camtasia – Helps users create high quality videos without prior experience. This tool records on-screen activity and also allows users to import from HD devices to edit and share video content

Jing – This free tool helps users share images and record videos from their screens. Users are able to quickly share this media to email, social and other various platforms.

Audacity – Record, edit and publish podcasts and interviews with this free software.

Podbean – Share and create podcasts with this tool that also lets you sell podcasts with no transaction fee.

ePodcast Creator – Control and customize every step of the podcast creation process with a full editing studio that creates a professional sound.

Content Distribution Tools

Brightcove – This provider of cloud content services offers an online video platform for adding custom video players to websites, social media profiles, and mobile destinations.

PR Newswire – Distribute news releases to a global media database of more than 700,000 journalists and blogger contacts, monitor traditional and social media, and engage in real time with journalists, bloggers, and other influencers.

SlideShare – Upload and share slide presentations, gain insight into who's viewing your presentations, collect business leads, and more.

Cadence9 – This unified solution for managing content marketing lets marketers plan content using an editorial calendar, assign tasks to team members, manage content creation and publishing workflow, and more.

Papershare – Cloud-based promotional tool for content marketers that distributes to multiple channels and alerts marketing and sales teams when content is published. Leads are also integrated into salesforce and marketing automation softwares.

Content Collaboration Tools

Compendium – Plan your content using Compendium's calendar-based tool, create efficiently placed content across multiple channels, and track the effectiveness of each piece of content.

Divvy – This platform combines web-based calendars, content management and online collaboration to help global content teams plan, schedule and produce any type of content across an organization.

GatherContent - Organize and streamline your website content using drag and drop features, create content guidelines, collaborate with a content team, and export content using this online collaboration tool.

Google Drive – Create, store, and share including spreadsheets, text documents, drawings, forms, and presentations.

Kapost - This content marketing platform allows marketers to collaborate, distribute, and analyze all content types within a single platform.

SocialCast – This collaboration tool organizes workflow into a single location accessible from anywhere on any device.

Marketing-AI – In this platform users are able to collaborate with team members in a calendar, build a content strategy using a framework and promote published content & measure its impact.

Curata – Easily find, organize & share relevant content for

your business to position your brand as an industry thought leader, increase brand visibility and generate leads.

Globalization/Localization of Content

Globalization of business is the change in a business from a company associated with a single country to one that operates in multiple countries and Localization is all about making the business compatible from a systems and process perspective to the local country.

You might be doing business in say 20 countries so when you create content for different channels now you need to translate the content in all the languages catering to the 20 countries. This makes the content management task which is already challenging to being more cumbersome. As a business you might want to centralize this across the enterprise as this is not just related to marketing but other functions like products, sales, services, finances and so on.

Localization tools

CloudWords – This translation management tool allows you to localize content by uploading it to a system and then selecting a vendor to translate it.

SmartLing- Speak to customers in their native language with this tool that automates the translation process by connecting content producers with translation professionals.

Translationcloud.net - This is a hub for hiring professionals who translate content to a variety of languages.

Phrase App – Translate content that is stored on websites,

mobile and desktop applications with this translation management software.

Crowd in – Manage the localization workflow process with this software that helps control the process, but also provides tools for translators to work more efficiently.

Conclusion

Content marketing is headed for an interesting future where embedded videos, interactive graphics, social integrations, SEO and mobile optimization, together with written content, will form the content marketers' mix. And the key is none of these can do wonders, it is the sum of the whole that will make the difference. Prepare a good content strategy and then execute towards it.

6. SOCIAL MEDIA MARKETING

Contents

1. Introduction

2. Advantages of Social Media

3. Blogging

4. Rise of Social Networks

5. Conclusion

81% of customers reach out to social networks for purchasing advice.

82% of the world's population can be reached by a social network.

Introduction

Social Media Marketing is all about marketing using social networking platforms like facebook, linkedin, twitter, youtube, pinterest etc. Social networking websites allow individuals to interact with one another and build relationships. When companies join these social channels, consumers can interact with them directly. That interaction can be more personal to users than traditional methods of outbound marketing & advertising.

Social media present great marketing opportunities for businesses of all sizes. You can use social media to:

- promote your brand and business

- tell prospects about your goods and services

- find out what customers think of your business

- attract new customers

- build stronger relationships with existing customers.

Some interesting metrics to understand :-

- 78% of salespeople who use social media outsell their peers

- 54% of salespeople who used social media tracked their social media usage back to at least one closed deal.

- 67% of B2B purchase cycles are completed before the buyer considers contacting the vendor; sales needs a way to engage online and earlier

- 70% of business technology buyers are at the RFP stage (request for proposal) by the time the vendor becomes aware of the opportunity – UBM Techweb.

Advantages of using social media

Social media marketing has many advantages:

- Broad reach : Social media can reach millions of people all around the world. 82% of the world's population can be reached by a social network.

- Ability to target particular groups : Many forms of social media (e.g. Facebook, Linkedin, Twitter, etc) allow businesses to target specific groups, often in particular locations.

- Free or low-cost : Many forms of social media are free for business, and paid options are usually low-cost.

- Personal : Social media allow you to communicate on a personal basis with individual customers and groups. 15% of people trust messages from companies vs 70% trust recommendations from people they know.

- Fast : You can quickly distribute information to many people. 81% of customers reach out to social networks for purchasing advice.

- Easy : You don't need high-level skills or computer equipment to participate in social media. The average person with a standard computer should have no difficulty.

Risks of using social media

Of course, marketing through social media also has its risks. These include:

- Wasted time and money for little or no tangible return. As of today, social media is widely used for brand awareness and not for selling directly through that.

- Negative publicity - negative reviews posted by some disgruntled employee or unhappy customers can reach far and wide.

- Legal problems if you don't follow privacy legislation and the laws regarding spam, copyright and other online issues.

It's important to be aware of these risks and to have strategies in place to avoid them if you decide to get involved in social media marketing.

Along with building social networks on standard platforms like facebook and twitter, it is also good idea to create and manage your own blogging which you can moderate more closely.

Blogging

Blog is an excellent marketing tool for businesses. It takes time to establish your blog but the results are well worth the effort. To get most out of your blog, you will need to set aside some time every week to write quality content. The benefits of a blog increase manifold as you increase your publishing frequency. Studies show that businesses that blog regularly are more than two times as likely to generate leads via their website as businesses that don't. It also builds trust in your business. Businesses who blog get 67% more leads than those who don't.

9 Most Common Business Blogging Mistakes

• Your blog is not hosted on your site

• You have not updated your blog in over a month

• You have not defined your blogging audience

• You aren't collecting email addresses on your blog

• You aren't offering an incentive to sign up

• You have no social sharing buttons on your blog

• You aren't promoting your blog posts

• You're using sorely outdated SEO tactics

• Your writing is hard to read. There's a helpful tool called

Hemingway (hemingwayapp.com) that can help making your writing easier to read.

There are two main steps you need to go through in order to set up a blog. The two steps:

1. Choose your preferred blogging platform. The chart below has a mix of self-hosting platforms and free blogging platform providers.

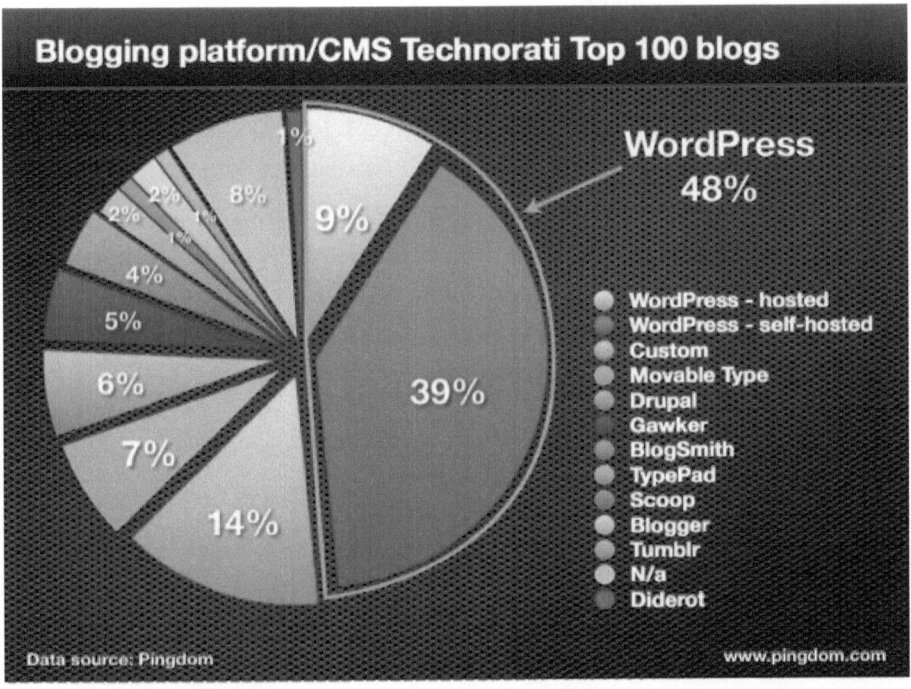

2. Choose whether you want to self-host and a paid domain, or get a free blog. WordPress, Tumblr and Blogger all offer free blogs for anyone. But it does have downsides like not having your domain name (eg: yourblog.wordpress.com or yourblog.blogspot.com etc), there will be content size limits on blogs and so on.

If you decide to self host then follow the 2 steps below

> Setting up a blog on your own domain (if you choose self-hosting and a custom domain). Here you might need some expertise to setup a blog linked to your website. Most website hosting providers do provide blogging software like wordpress, drupal, joomla etc.

> Designing your blog. This could be fun where you can configure your blog.

Rise of social networks

Social Media has overtaken porn as the #1 activity on the web. We all knew social media was popular, but this popular? Apparently it's the most common thing we do online.

The percentage of online adults who use social networking sites has steadily risen. As of January 2014, 74% of all online adults use social networking sites.

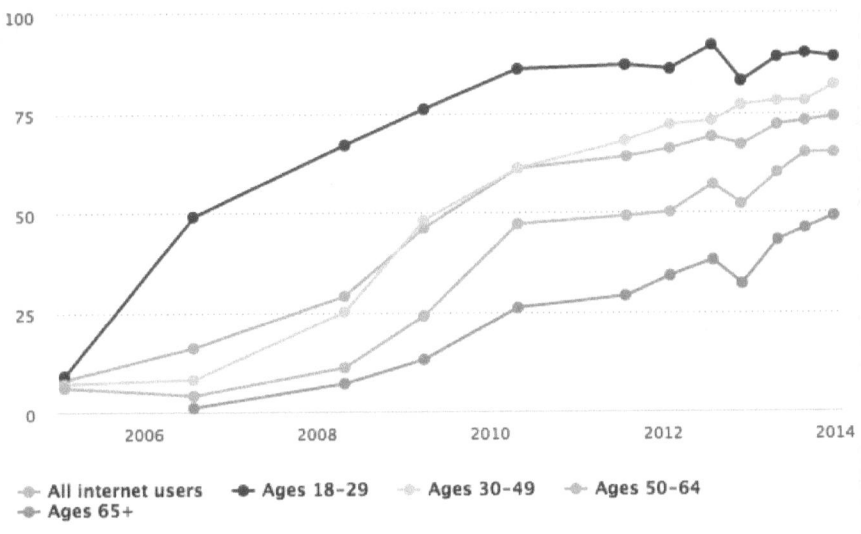

400 mil snapchat photos and videos are received every day

100 hours of video is uploaded to youtube every minute

Pinterest sharing content grew 19% in 2013, Facebook only grew 15%, while twitter fell to 8%

FB is seeing a decrease in daily users "specifically among teens"

Google+ is second in terms of monthly visitors behind FB

Per Avinash Kaushik, Entrepreneur and digital marketing evangelist, four major social media metrics were designed as a foil to the somewhat popular notions of chasing vanity metrics like follower count, number of posts, and other low-value statistics.

What matters is everything that happens after you post / tweet / participate!

Did you grab attention? Did you deliver delight? Did you cause people to want to share? Did you initiate a discussion? Did you cause people to take an action? Did your participation deliver economic value?

To that end, Kaushik's four metrics are as follows:

1. Conversation rate – The number of conversations per post. On Facebook, Google+, and LinkedIn, it's comments. On Twitter, it's replies.

2. Amplification rate – The number of reshares or retweets per post.

3. Applause rate – Retweets, Likes, +1s, etc.

4. Economic value – The sum of short-term revenue, long-term revenue, and cost savings

Key social media services

Different types of social media are good for different marketing activities. Some popular social media platforms :

Facebook : This social media platform has over a billion users and lets users connect with friends, share links, photos, videos, and events, join groups, and more.

Twitter : With over half a billion registered users, Twitter lets users post messages of up to 140 characters, share photos and videos, create custom lists, send direct messages, and more.

Pinterest : Pinterest users share and tag images and videos on customizable boards, follow brands and individuals, "repin" images, and more. Pinterest has nearly 50 million users.

YouTube : An online video-hosting service that lets people share their videos.

LinkedIn : A business-focused online network that includes features such as sharing links, adding connections, joining groups, writing recommendations, searching for connections by company, industry, skills, and more.

Blogs : Internet sites that contain a series of entries or 'posts' about topics of interest to the author, much like an online 'diary'.

Google+ : Google+ (or Google Plus) is a social networking and identity service that is owned and operated by Google Inc. Google+ is second in terms of monthly visitors behind Facebook.

Offerpop : Offerpop is a social media platform for businesses to recruit, engage and convert customers.

Coupon sites : Websites that offer discount coupons for goods, services and events like Groupon etc.

Online photo-sharing services : Websites that allow users to store, organize and share their photo collections like instagram, flickr, shutterfly etc.

Location-based marketing sites - websites that deliver targeted marketing messages to customers in particular locations, through mobile devices such as smartphones and tablets.

Customer review sites - websites that feature customer reviews of goods and services.

Conclusion

82% of the world's population can be reached by a social network so it is high time to get to them with this low cost method.

Focus on the following through social media :

- promote your brand and business

- tell prospects about your goods and services

- find out what customers think of your business

- attract new customers

- build stronger relationships with existing customers

At a minimum setup the following :

Create and moderate Google+, Facebook, Linkedin, Twitter and/or Youtube channels. Check out videos on youtube on how you would create and manage these networks. Keep an eye on other channels and look at expanding when the time comes. Have company marketing content posted on a regular basis through these channels.

Create your own blogging site which is closely moderated with rating, point systems, gamification etc to make it interesting. Have leaders post content on a regular basis. Please note that a stale blogging site is better than not having a blogging site.

Don't be surprised that this does not convert into revenue immediately since in most cases it will not but it will spread the good message far and wide which will bring business in the long run. This is a new channel and everyday there are breakthrough technologies getting innovated.

If you're struggling to make your strategy work, or you just want some advice, you don't have to go it alone. Since 93% of marketers are using social media for business, you can probably find someone to give you a hand. Mobile phone usage has also become beneficial for social media marketing. Today, most cell phones have social networking capabilities: individuals are notified of any happenings on social networking sites through their cell phones, in real-time.

7. MOBILE MARKETING

Contents

1. Why Mobile Marketing

2. Location Based Marketing

3. Conclusion

91% of adults have their mobile phones within arms reach 24x7. 47% of mobile users want retailers to send coupons to their devices when they are in or near the physical locations. Now there are more active mobile devices than human beings around the world.

Why Mobile Marketing

As of October, 2014, for the first time ever, there are more gadgets in the world than there are people, including a growing number that only communicate with other machines, according to data from digital analysts at GSMA Intelligence.

The number of active mobile devices and human beings crossed over somewhere around the 7.19 billion mark.

What a difference 8 years make. St. Peter's Square in 2005 vs. 2013. This came from a tweet where the 2013 picture was the crowd watching as the new Pope Francis speaks for the first time after he was elected and the 2005 picture is that of Pope John Paul II's death when his body was carried across the square. The picture speaks for itself on the increase of mobile.

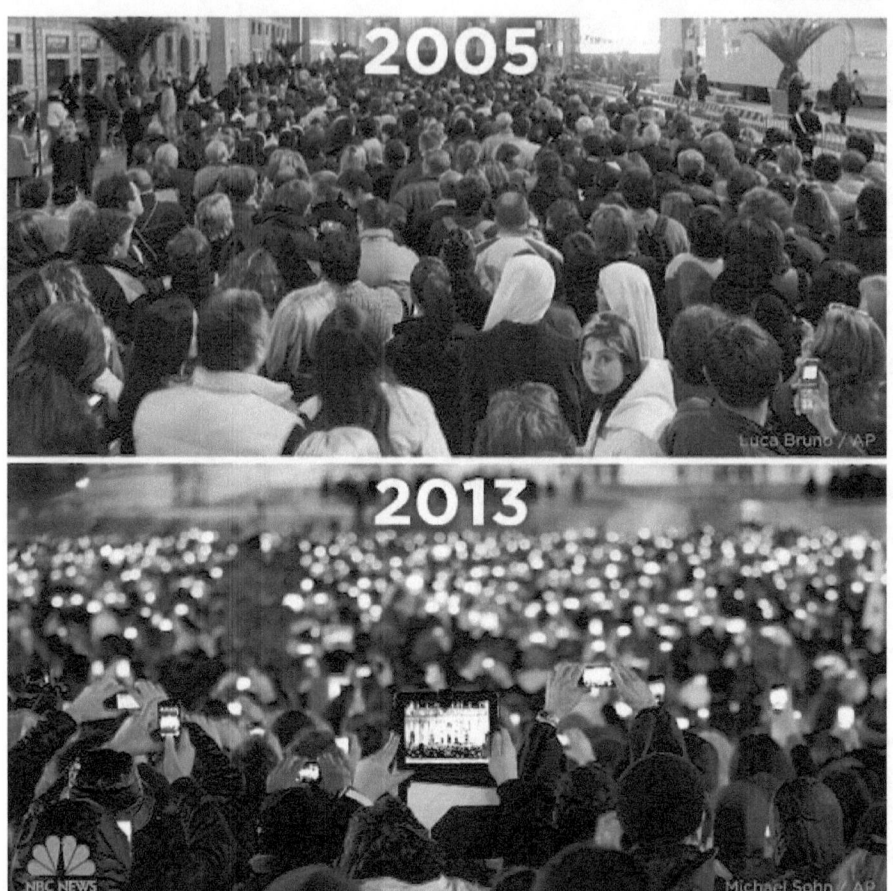

Gadgets like tablets, smartphones and not-so-smart phones are multiplying five times faster than we are, with our population growing at a rate of about two people per second, or 1.2% annually.

"No other technology has impacted us like the mobile phone. It's the fastest growing manmade phenomenon ever -- from zero to 7.2 billion in three decades," said Kevin Kimberlin, Chairman of Spencer Trask & Co.

Half of all local searches are performed on mobile devices.

After less than a decade of existence, smartphones and

tablets this year will draw more money from advertisers than the centuries-old newspaper industry or the nearly century-old radio sector, a sign of just how rapidly technology is transforming media habits. Hence the concept of "Mobile-First Marketing". Most analysts agree that brands will have to put more thought into leveraging mobile technology in the coming months in order to create experiences that serve consumers' needs.

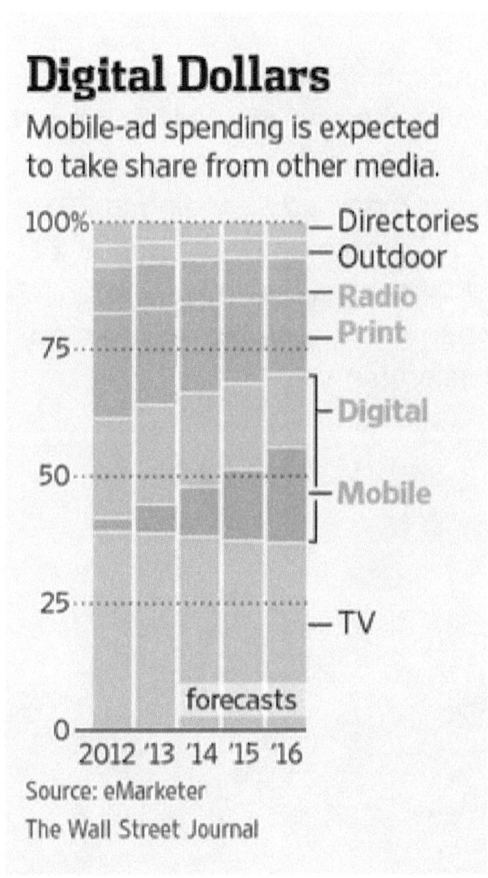

Digital Dollars

Mobile-ad spending is expected to take share from other media.

Source: eMarketer

The Wall Street Journal

Research firm eMarketer estimates that spending on mobile advertising, which includes both smartphones and tablets, will soar 83% to nearly $18 billion by end of 2014. Newspapers will draw nearly $17 billion, while radio will bring in $15.5 billion.

American adults now spend almost a quarter of their media time on mobile devices, eMarketer estimates, yet this year's spending growth will raise mobile's share of the ad market to only 9.8%. By contrast, American adults spend only 2% of their media time reading newspapers but ad spending for the sector hangs just under 10% of the overall market, eMarketer estimates.

U.S. ad firms and marketers will spend about $1.5 billion on mobile video ads by the end of 2014, up from the $722 million spent in 2013. Mobile video ads accounted for nearly 19 percent of all digital video ad spending in 2013, a number that will climb to nearly 26 percent by the end of 2014, according to eMarketer principal analyst David Hallerman. "And by the year 2018, the number will quadruple to over $6 billion. This is huge growth," Hallerman said.

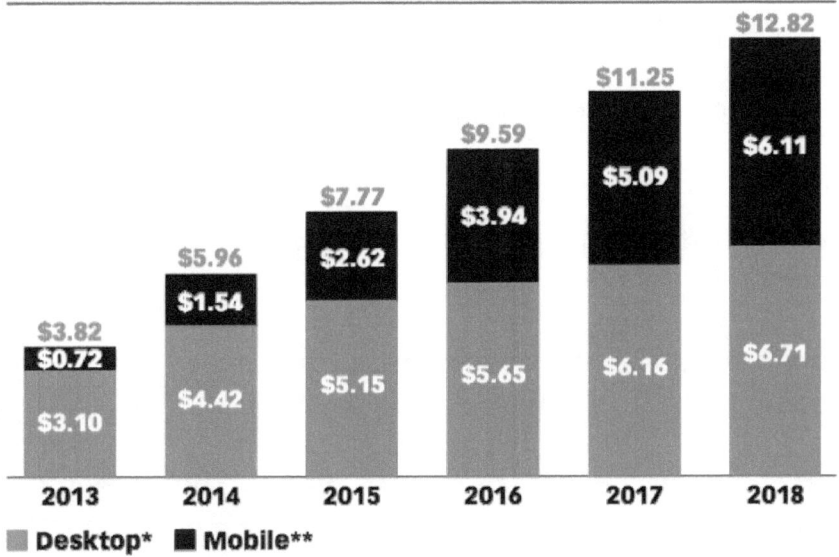

US Digital Video Ad Spending, by Device, 2013-2018
billions

Note: *includes advertising that appears on desktop and laptop computers;
**includes mobile phones and tablets; includes in-banner, in-stream and
in-text
Source: eMarketer, Sep 2014

178334   www.**eMarketer**.com

Location based marketing

Marketing campaign organizers attempt to adapt their message to the people who are likely to view them. The advertisements you view in a large city, for example, are likely to vary from those you may see in a rural setting. This is because businesses make educated guesses on the socioeconomic nature of people based on where they're located. For instance, marketers who target airports know that their target audience has enough financial resources to travel and has time on their hands while waiting to board a flight or pass through security, so these marketers adapt their billboards, digital displays and fliers to the particular characteristics of that audience.

74% of smartphone owners use location based services

47% of mobile users want retailers to send coupons to their devices when they are in or near the physical locations

91% of adults have their mobile phones within arms reach 24x7.

Location targeted campaigns will continue to increase reaching an ad spend of 5.8 Billion by 2016

There are a number of location-based strategies, which can be broadly split into "Push" and "Pull" marketing.

Push methods use Bluetooth or SMS alerts when consumers are near to a store or venue, though there is the downside that customers may find these tactics invasive, and would therefore be less receptive to marketing messages.

A pull strategy is a better approach, and this means using consumers' locations and search habits to serve up information and offers that can entice into local outlets.

Apps could also be used by cinemas, theaters, and other venues to target consumers in the local area and provide them with last minute offers on tickets.

With so many apps out there, it can be a challenge to get yours onto a consumer's smartphone, so you need to be innovative and offer compelling reasons for people to download and use your apps.

Conclusion

Mobile marketing is the new wave and with 91% of adults

have their mobile phones within arms reach 24x7, you need to start keeping a close watch on this. Some of the potential strategies that you could embark upon :

Mobile Responsive Web properties and mobile friendly content. Have your entire website be mobile responsive. This makes it easy for users to lookup content on your site and click through the CTA.

Location based marketing - Based on your business use consumers' locations and search habits to serve up information and offers.

Creation of mobile apps. Come up with innovative ideas on getting your customers to install your mobile app.

8. ANALYTICS

Contents

1. Introduction

2. Tracking the Data that matters

3. Predictive Analytics

4. Conclusion

Measure what matters.

Measure the past and the present, to build strategies and predict the future of the business.

Introduction

Marketing Analytics evaluate the success of your marketing initiatives by measuring performance (e.g., SEO Vs Paid Search Vs Email Campaigns) using important business metrics, such as ROI, marketing attribution and overall marketing effectiveness. In other words, it tells you how your marketing programs are really performing. Marketing analytics gathers data from across all marketing channels and consolidates it into a common marketing view.

The marketing performance can be visualized as a typical

marketing funnel with the closed-loop reporting data as shown in the diagram above. Based on a study conducted by SiriusDecisions, the average closed deals per 1000 inquiries are 2.89 whereas this number for best in class companies is 14.23. What is your company's numbers ?

Building analytics is a key activity since Marketing has been an area where there has been innovative ways coming up so frequently that if you don't keep a pulse on the latest, your methods will be obsolete and ineffective losing ground to your competitors. Newspaper was once the ideal channel for marketers which got replaced by TV and then the online space and more recently the emerging mobility channel. If you dig further within each channel there is lot of innovation happening.

What can marketing analytics do with historic data, current data and future predictions.

Past : By using marketing analytics to report on the past, you can answer such questions as: Which campaign elements generated the most revenue last quarter? How did email campaign A perform against direct mail campaign B? How many leads did we generate from social media campaign C?

Present : Marketing analytics enables you to determine how your marketing initiatives are performing right now by answering questions like: How are our customers engaging with us? Which channels do our most profitable customers prefer? Who is talking about our brand on social media sites, and what are they saying?

Future : Marketing analytics can also deliver data-driven predictions that you can use to influence the future by answering such questions as: How can we turn short-term wins into loyalty and ongoing engagement? How will adding 10 more sales people in under-performing regions affect revenue? Which cities should we target next using our current portfolio? How can we expedite the buyer's journey?

Tracking the Data That Matters

Neil Patel, founder of CrazyEgg and KISSMetrics, has a very straight forward philosophy on data collection and analysis : **Measure what matters**. With metrics, it's easy to get caught up in vanity metrics. Vanity metrics are the things that make you feel good and may even give you some idea of what's happening, but they're not really indicative of what's happening to your business which are KPIs like

- Visits to your site
- Page views
- Number of newsletter subscribers
- Followers on social media
- Bounce rate
- Time spent on your site

Tracking these are pretty easy and seeing growth in these numbers over time can be a useful trend, but for the most part, you're instead looking for the kinds of metrics that show action.

Useful data tracking comes down to evaluating:

- Who is coming to your site, and what are those people doing once they get there?

- What channels are driving buying customers?

- Who is converting?

- What conversions are deepening relationships?

- What conversions are driving revenue?

- Who is buying multiple times?

- What's your lifetime customer value?

One of the other challenges with Digital Marketing has been that it is all fragmented in most companies. There needs to be an oversight across all channel performance, what is the channel attribution, where to invest and by how much and so forth.

Predictive Analytics

Predictive Analytics is a way to predict the future using data from the past.

Lack of good data is the most common barrier to organizations seeking to employ predictive analytics. To make predictions about what customers will buy in the future, for example, you need to have good data on who is buying, what they have bought in the past, the attributes of those products (attribute-based predictions are often more accurate than the "people who buy this also buy this" type of model), and perhaps some demographic attributes of the customer (age, gender, residential location, socioeconomic status, etc.). If you have multiple channels or customer touchpoints, you need to make sure that they capture data on customer purchases in the same way your previous channels did in order to aggregate.

Regression analysis, a field of statistics, in its various forms is the primary tool that organizations use for predictive analytics. It works like this in general: An analyst hypothesizes that a set of independent variables (say, gender, income, visits to a website) are statistically correlated with the purchase of a product for a sample of customers. The analyst performs a regression analysis to see just how correlated each variable is; this usually requires some iteration to find the right combination of variables and the best model. Let's say that the analyst succeeds and finds that each variable in the model is important in explaining the product purchase, and together the variables explain a lot of variation in the product's sales. Using that regression equation, the analyst can then use the regression coefficients—the degree to which each variable affects the purchase behavior—to create a score predicting the likelihood of the purchase.

Here are a few good questions to ask your analysts:

- Can you tell me something about the source of data you used in your analysis?

- Are you sure the sample data are representative of the population?

- Are there any outliers in your data distribution? How did they affect the results?

- What assumptions are behind your analysis?

- Are there any conditions that would make your assumptions invalid?

Businesses collect vast amounts of real-time customer data and predictive analytics uses this historical data, combined with customer insight, to predict future events. Predictive analytics enable organizations to use big data (both stored and real-time) to move from a historical view to a forward-looking perspective of the customer.

Predictive analytics does not tell you what will happen in the future. It forecasts what might happen in the future with an acceptable level of reliability, and includes what-if scenarios and risk assessment.

Conclusion

There is an explosion of data in different forms.

- 400 mil snapchat photos and videos are received every day

- 100 hours of video is uploaded to youtube every minute

- 2/3rd of the world's data will be video by 2017

- If your business is one of the many that's struggling with a gap in analytical capacity, it's time to have a frank internal conversation about which data gaps can dramatically improve your business. Start by evaluating your current data state, what metrics you should be tracking, and what cultural impact adding data to your process is likely to have. Then you'll be ready to take a deeper dive into understanding different analytical resources and technologies available to you.

9. OMNI CHANNEL PERSONALIZATION

Contents

1. Introduction
2. Buyer Journey/Customer Lifecycle
3. Personalization
4. Persona and Profile
5. Omni Channel
6. Business Architecture Approach
7. Measure the KPIs
8. Marketing to Sales
9. Conclusion

Consumers take a multi device path to purchase.

90% of consumers start a task on one device and finish it on another

Introduction

Per Gartner, Customer experience was the top marketing technology investment, averaged 18% of total marketing budget in 2014, and is ranked the #1 innovation project for 2015. Also 89% of companies plan to compete primarily on the basis of customer experience by 2016.

The term "omni channel" may be a marketing buzzword, but it refers to a significant shift. Marketo, one of the leading Marketing Automation providers gives a solid explanation of why marketers need to think Omni-Channel: "Marketers now need to provide a seamless experience, regardless of channel or device. Consumers can now engage with a company in a physical store, on an online website or mobile app, through a catalog, or through social media. They can access products and services by calling a company on the phone, by using an app on their mobile smartphone, or with a tablet, a laptop, or a desktop computer. Each piece of the consumer's experience should be consistent and complementary. "

Omni channel is not just a fancier name for multichannel. In the words of John Bowden, Senior VP of Customer Care at Time Warner Cable: "Multi-channel is an operational view – how you allow the customer to complete transactions in each channel. Omni-channel, however, is viewing the experience through the eyes of your customer, orchestrating the customer experience across all channels so that it is seamless, integrated, and consistent. Omni channel anticipates that customers may start in one channel and move to another as they progress to a resolution. Making these complex 'hand-offs' between channels must be fluid for the customer. "

This matters because marketing today is more about

outcomes than interactions. Popularity measures in social are a good example – you know, all the "like" metrics. According to a recent ANA study, more than 80 percent of U.S. marketers rely on popularity-based metrics, such as likes and shares, to measure the effectiveness of their social content. However, popularity is no substitute for strategy. What matters is not how many people like your pictures of kittens, whitepaper downloads, or clever tweets, but the outcomes of those interactions – usually sales, loyalty, product reviews, up-sells, cross-sells etc.

Reiterating some of the key challenges :

For large technology purchases 7.2 decisions makers on average can touch or influence the decision.

The hardest thing about B2B selling today is that customers don't need you the way they used to per Harvard Business Review.

Two-thirds to 90% of the buying cycle is completed before a B2B buyer ever speaks with a sales rep. – Forrester

Business buyers spend just 21% of buying cycle in conversations with salespeople, instead spending 23% of the time in conversations with peers and colleagues and 56% of the buying cycle searching for and engaging with content – IDG Connect

Buyer Journey/Customer Lifecycle

Customers want simple, consistent, and relevant experiences across all interactions throughout the lifecycle. Exceptional customer experiences throughout the lifecycle create the loyalty, advocacy, and repeat business that drives success. Integrated and well-designed solutions are the key to sustaining this high level of customer experience, driving the customer acquisition, retention, and efficiency that make leading companies successful.

Whether a consumer or business, customers move through a closed-loop, continuous customer experience lifecycle as they engage and interact with your company and brand over time like an infinity loop.

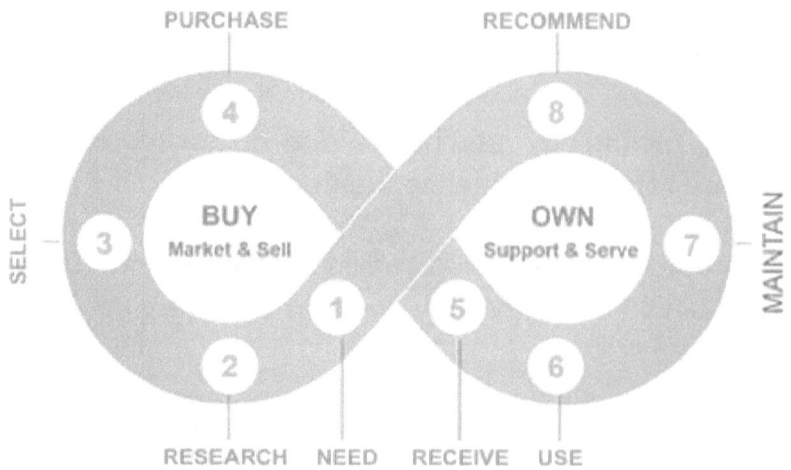

Based on a whitepaper from Oracle on "Customer Experience Reference Architecture", achieving great customer experience requires a complete, robust customer experience solution that delivers consistent information and functionality across all points of interaction throughout the entire customer lifecycle. In today's connected world, the customer experience spans multiple different touch points throughout the customer lifecycle. Figure below illustrates an example of how a customer could move through multiple different touch points during the buying process.

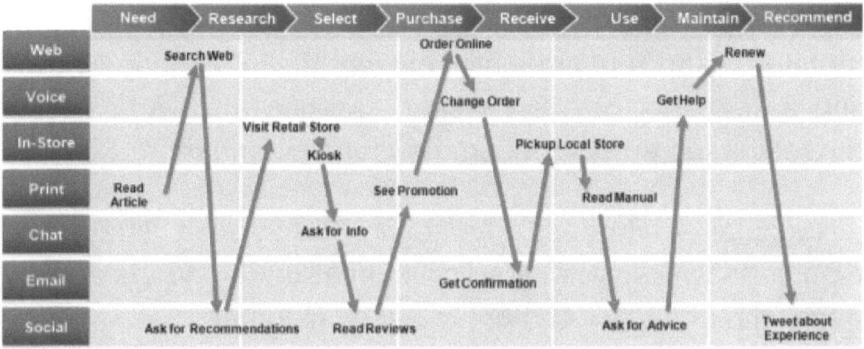

Based on the experience he/she might upgrade, renew and/or buy new products and/or service.

Personalization

Personalization has made its way into just about every aspect of digital marketing, but this year will bring a heightened use of algorithms to hyper-personalize ads. Retargeting and location targeting will pair up in more marketing campaigns to deliver a cohesive consumer experience that anticipates and responds to the customer's every need.

Personalized Marketing, is also called marketing to the Segment of One. Amazon is a classic example of a company that performs "One to One Marketing" by offering users targeted offers and related products. Having a knowledge of the consumer's preferences enables suggesting specific products and promotions to each consumer.

Tools for personalization :

Demandbase – Create targeted, relevant conversations with buyers at every stage, personalize the web experience, segment and analyze companies and more using this B2B marketing tool.

Monetate – Turn real-time into relevant digital experiences by taking a snapshot of every visitor, creating multivariate tests and rules-based product recommendations, and more.

40 Nuggets – Harness marketing automation strategies, audience-analytics, and predictive intelligence to personally engage with and tailor content to each customer.

Idio – Improve content marketing strategy by examining specific customer interests and increasing the engagement of content.

Profile and Personas

When you get started with a company they ask you to fill in a form to identify yourselves each time you login. You might be going to the site to try out their software for evaluation or downloading a whitepaper or accessing other content that is of interest to you. This information does go into the enterprise systems which centralizes it. The trick to getting the good amount of user information is progressive profiling.

Progressive profiling technology, a feature that is usually an extension of dynamic form fields, allows you to set up iterative forms that enable you to designate which questions appear based on what you already know about a particular lead. That way, every time a lead fills out a form, you are progressively collecting valuable new information about them while keeping your forms short and easy to complete. This enables you to build up the amount of information, or intelligence, you collect about your individual leads without causing more friction in the conversion process. Ultimately, progressive profiling technology enables you to collect the right information from your leads -- at the right times. You can now leverage this profile data to start identifying the personas interested in the company's products and services.

With personas, businesses can be more strategic in catering to each audience, internalize the customer that they are trying to attract, and target them more specifically.

You want to know who the person is, what they value, and how best to speak to them. Here is a quick overview on what you should include in your marketing persona template:

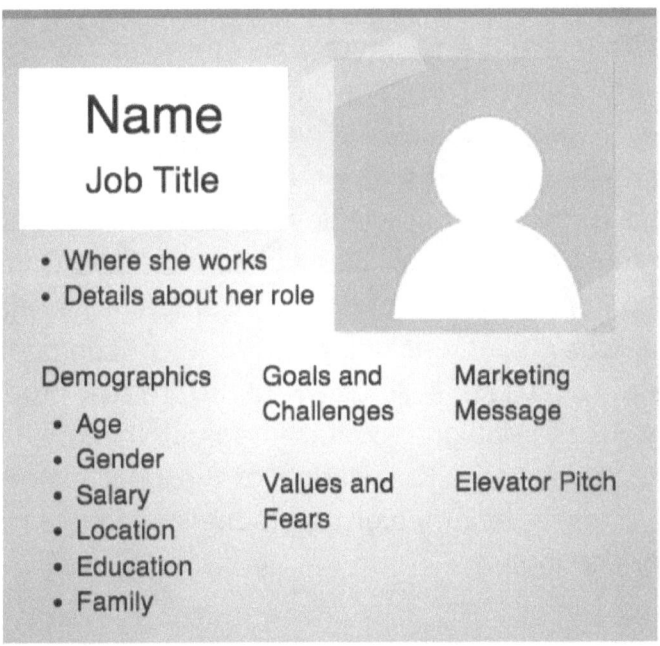

Marketing personas will help you identify with your audience and better solve their problems. And when you solve their problems, everyone wins. The results will be a better experience for the customer and a more engaged user for your business.

Based on your business you could try "Need Center clustering". Create an additional hierarchy element that clusters the Contacts into specific groups based on their business/product needs. Focuses on where specific buying decisions are made: combination of hierarchical (parent vs subsidiary/office) and product need dimensions. Mostly applies to the medium/larger organizations. Where applicable, marketing campaigns will be targeted to specific Need Centers. Need Center is a Persona, overlaid with a specific product need.

While creating a contact in the marketing systems, you can create "Unchained Person ID" i.e. create a Person ID that follows an individual, not a job. Person IDs will be mapped to Contact IDs (current and future), and through the Contact ID to the current employer. Develop an identity management framework to define which data will be collected and stored on the Person ID (unrelated to the current employer) and Contact ID (related to the current employer) levels. Examples of the Person – level data: Name, Certification(s), Past Contact IDs, Product purchase/usage history, Campaign engagement history (at past jobs), including content consumption, event attendance, etc. This will allow us to retain product and engagement (campaign, content, sales) history, when a Contact changes jobs. Knowledge of the past history will be used in message/campaign personalization as well as propensity scoring.

Omni Channel

To impact true digital transformation, we must stop thinking about digital in the context of nontraditional versus traditional advertising, inbound versus outbound marketing, one channel over other and so on. Silos are created through the annual budget process, as well as legacy organizational structures. As digital marketing gains substantial credibility and investment in large organizations, there is the opportunity for digital marketers to influence the broader customer journey, including the offer, customer service, and post-purchase care. These are the memorable moments that will give customers a reason to keep coming back.

Consumers take a multi device path to purchase. 90% of consumers start a task on one device and finish it on another. Here's a chart from Telco 2.0 Research, illustrating the frequency of multi-device paths to purchase:

Consumers take a multi-device path to purchase

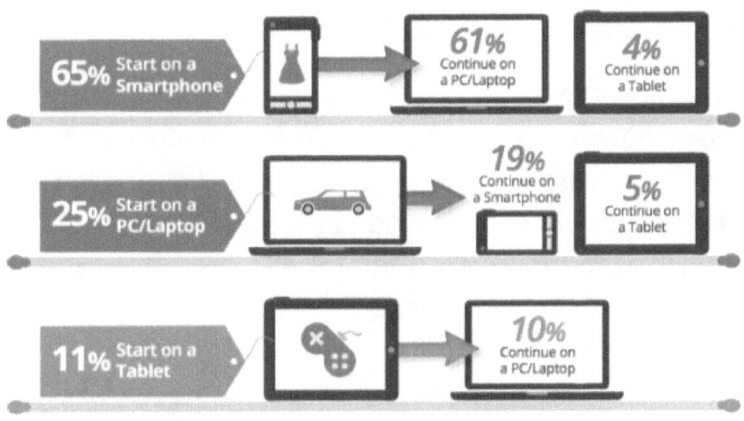

There are ways to bring your marketing more into the customer-centric omni channel approach without boiling the ocean. Try these four:

Be more aware of how customers are interacting with your brands, owned, paid, and earned media, and customer service centers today. Are there simple opportunities to listen more strategically and respond to customer input and interaction? Focus on the channels where you have the most control – search, display, email, customer support – and slowly work your way over to a more holistic strategy. Tackle one set of synergies at a time. Typically, digital channels like mobile and email have high synergy, but so do display and email. The right combination will be unique to your business.

Get serious about attribution for all of your channels. Without it, omni channel strategies will always overemphasize the last touch.

Start with mobile. It is the common denominator for nearly every customer contact and is increasingly these "lean in" experiences that both introduce consumers to a brand or offer, and engage them in loyalty activities.

Think about interactions. Customers may already be interacting with your brand across channels, and most likely they are not doing it in a linear, neat, and streamlined way. Branded interactions are more like "shared experiences" than they are a step-by-step process.

Make sure you are capturing every movement of your prospects and customers across all devices and channels. Analyze this data from the lens of your personas. This will help you identify some key propensity models based on the personas. If you do not identify the propensity models, then you have wrongly classified your personas. Identify short and long term propensity models. This will be a cumbersome process but do due diligence till you identify the models. Once you have the propensity models then you need to work on personalizing the users experience based on this model across all channels and devices. Keep measuring and provide a balanced scorecard for your marketing business on a frequent basis to understand if anything is changing. As the company grows into different products or different business models these will change and you need to change with it.

A high level omni channel personalization architecture :

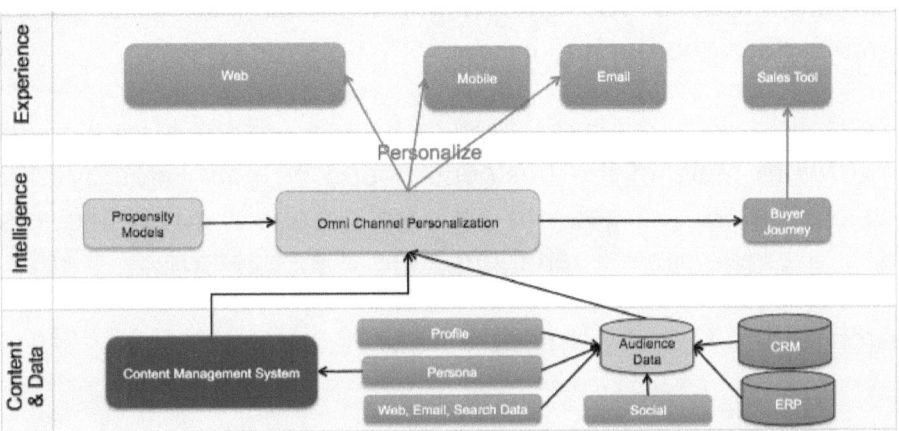

A simplified way to break down the omni channel personalization capability architecturally is Content & Data, Intelligence and Experience.

In the Content & Data section, we need to have a content management system used to author, package, publish and manage marketing content or assets. The blue boxes depict the existing systems or data which needs to be aggregated into Audience Data. This Audience data gets fed to the next layer called Intelligence. The Omni channel Personalization capability works more like a rules engine taking in the audience data and the propensity models to derive the content from the content management system that needs to be rendered to the experience layer be it the Web, Mobile or Email. In the intelligence layer also resides the Buyer journey capability which extracts the same information for a sales person as he/she is working through converting a lead.

Business Architecture Approach

Depending on your business which might be in the midst of a fragmented digital marketing capability experience, where most businesses are, and not sure how to move to what matters most to you, you might want to take a business architecture approach to it.

You can use a business architecture approach to getting to the future state of the business based on your strategy and vision. Before we get into how we go about doing this lets define a few things. Even though this is a larger topic

Architecture is a way to keep things

- **Simple**

- **Consistent**

- **Scalable**

Business Architecture is a framework and set of methodologies for using architecture-led planning techniques to simplify and focus complex decision-making for strategic business investments.

Business blueprint is a simplified view of the organization which helps in identifying what to build based on the organization's strategy and goals. It helps to avoid redundancies, achieve clarity and simplify planning.

Business Capability is "what" a business does at its core. This differs from the "how" things are done which defines the business process. Business Capability is delivered through a set of business processes. IT Application or systems are created to automate the business process.

For eg : "Lead Management" is a business capability, whereas "Create Email Lead" is a business process. As an organization we can either use a marketing automation tool to automate the creation of lead or keep it to the manual process of capturing the lead.

Hope this does ground the concept. Certainly this is a pretty loaded subject and new in the industry that needs more explanation but in this context looking to keep things at this level and get into how do we go about leveraging a business architecture approach for transforming the digital marketing plan of action.

This is a simple 4 step process to achieve this.

- **Identify Strategy and goals.** Identify and document your business strategy and goals. A sample strategy could be to accelerate the buyer's journey. The goals can be for example double your marketing sourced opportunities in 1 year or double the conversion rate of your sourced opportunities in 2 quarters or reduce the time to market of your new products by 50% in 1 year etc. Make sure your goals are SMART (Specific, Measurable, Attainable, Relevant and Time Bound).

- **Identify the current capability.** You need to capture your current state business capabilities. You could have these capabilities in multiple levels as a capability map. Keep in mind business capability is all about the "what" the business does at its core. In order to arrive at these capabilities you might want to interview your business stakeholders to make sure you understand what are significant capabilities that stand out for your business. Decompose your business capabilities into multiple logical levels. There is no perfect right or wrong on the capability map, it is basically making sure you understand how all the capabilities fit together to make the whole. A guideline to keep in mind is business capability is technology agnostic and unique within an enterprise.

- **Identify the capability gap to meet your goal.** This is where you map your goals to the capabilities to arrive at a heat map depicting potential gap in the so called future state Capability map. An example future state capability map is shown below.

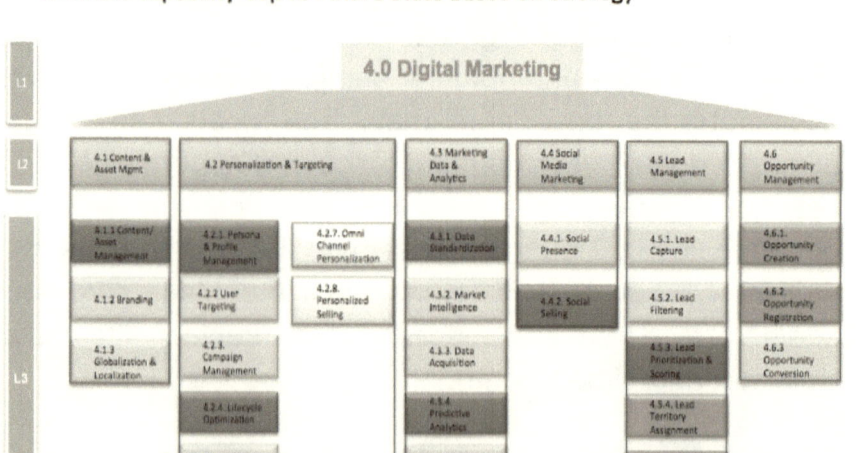

- **Prioritize capabilities and create roadmap.** Prioritize the capabilities in a 2X2 with one axis on criticality and the other on change/cost. You can look at prioritization criteria which matters to you with a mapping of those to the strategy so you can rate each capability accordingly. Finally put those onto a roadmap of initiatives to execute upon.

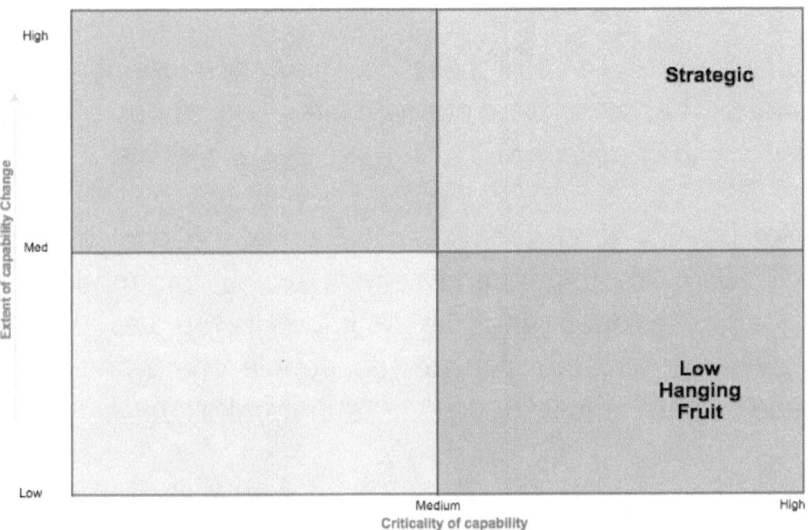

Once you do this for your organization, the next time there is a change to your strategy, then you only need to perform steps 3 and 4.

Measure the KPIs

Per Avinash Kaushik, the Key Performance Indicators to die for:

- Conversion Rate : Remember that the average website conversion rate usually is around 2%. So this is the fastest way to the heart of why your website mostly exists, but there is a lot more you should plan on worrying about in the future.

- Average Order Value (AOV) : For most companies there is a lot of effort spent in the area of onsite merchandizing (working on cross-sells and up-sells and what not). Awesomeness of all that work can be detected in by measuring AOV. That makes it a very good measure of success for site effectiveness.

- Days & Visits To "Purchase" : They measure the true customer behavior on your website, how long it takes someone to complete an Outcome on your website.

- Visitor Loyalty & Visitor Recency : Loyalty can also be a great way to understand effectiveness of marketing campaigns – deep analysis to know if you are driving behavior beyond the sign up (do people come back and "friend" others or just "nudge" or "super poke" :)).

- Task Completion Rate : Only 2% of your website visitors (for most websites) will ever convert on your website. How do you know why the other 98% visited your site and find ways in which your site is letting them down. Most people who visit your website are there for purposes you did not create it, this is how you find out.

- Share of Search : The web is the most frictionless environment in the universe and you compete the the fortune 500 company, you compete with the SMB and you compete with your neighbor's dog who has started his own facebook clone. You could use Compete.com to measure.

In order to measure the KPIs it is important that you are capturing the data in a way that can be easily reported upon.

You can leverage big data products or if you are trying to build some in house custom capability you need to capture the data accordingly. Capture audit trail information all along across channels and across content into a repository and provide a integrated view across. Decide which other information you want to collect, and turn on the audit trail of those. Figure out which KPIs relate to each piece of content. For instance, do you need to track number of email subscribers per piece of content? Calculate a baseline for each metric so you can understand what is performing above or below average. Create a balanced scorecard that you analyze on a frequent basis with your management team. This will provide you early insights into the trends so any strategic changes can be made early on.

Marketing to Sales

A prospect may click on to an email and fill a form with his contact information creating a lead that is captured in the system. This lead is then nurtured all the way to converting him/her to a customer. The marketing automation tools manage the process of acquiring contacts, capturing the lead, moving lead to opportunity and finally closing the opportunity by selling.

Most marketing automation tools do a fairly good job. Ideally, marketing automation is software and tactics that allow companies to nurture prospects with highly personalized, useful content that helps convert prospects to customers and turn customers into delighted customers.

Finally, Marketing is about generating demand for the sales team to convert. While generating demand is a good problem to solve, it is equally challenging to convert the growing demand to sale. Both can be looked upon as two sides of a coin.

Conclusion

Your customers expect a consistent, relevant, personalized and seamless buying experience. Your internal applications and systems need to support a disciplined approach to customer experience. We have now entered the age of the customer. Customers are making decisions that often bypass your employees and interact directly with their peers and social networks.

Creating great customer experiences starts with knowing exactly who your customers are and their needs, and providing the best recommendations based on their history with your company, as well as what you have learned through their social presence. You need to connect and personalize their experiences as they travel across touch points and engage with your brand.

Marketing today is more about outcomes than interactions. Outcomes are what omni channel marketing is all about, putting the customer at the center of the brand experience so that engagement turns into revenue and loyalty. Get started today to understand and learn more about your customers and provide the ultimate experience for them and your business.

ABOUT THE AUTHOR

Sudhir Sreedharan is an enterprise business architect having over 20 years of experience in the high tech industry working for giants like Cisco, HP and more recently VMware. In the recent past he has been introduced to Digital Marketing which led him to do a lot of analysis and eventually write this book. This is his first venture into writing a book. The contents of this book is based on his research of a lot of information collected from online media, his experience and other books.

www.ingramcontent.com/pod-product-compliance
Lightning Source LLC
Chambersburg PA
CBHW022111170526
45157CB00004B/1587